Lofts

Lofts

Edited by Ana Cristina G. Cañizares

An Imprint of HarperCollins*Publishers*

Publisher: **Paco Asensio**

Editor-in-chief: **Haike Falkenberg**

Editorial Coordination and Text: **Ana Cristina G. Cañizares**

Art Director: **Mireia Casanovas Soley**

Graphic Design: **Emma Termes**

Layout: **Ignasi Gracia Blanco**

Copy-editing: **Karen Capria and Gyda Arber**

Copyright © 2003 by HARPER DESIGN INTERNATIONAL and LOFT Publications

First published in 2003 by:
Harper Design International, an imprint of HarperCollins Publishers
10 East 53rd Street
New York, NY 10022

Distributed throughout the world by:
HarperCollins International
10 East 53rd Street
New York, NY 10022
Tel: (212) 207-7000
Fax: (212) 207-7654

HarperCollins books may be purchased for educational, business, or sales promotional use.
For information, please write:
Special Markets Department
HarperCollins Publishers Inc.
10 East 53rd Street
New York, NY 10022

Editorial project:

2003 © **LOFT** Publications
Via Laietana 32, 4th Of. 92.
08003 Barcelona. Spain
Tel.: +34 932 688 088
Fax: +34 932 687 073
loft@loftpublications.com
www.loftpublications.com

Library of Congress Control Number: 2003103503
ISBN: 0-06-054471-6
D.L.: B-28.211-03
Printed by:
Anman Gràfiques del Vallès, Spain
www.anman.com
Third Printing, 2004

008 **INTRODUCTION**

012 **LEVELS**

014 **Zartoshty Loft** Stephen Chung

018 **Inspired by Ice** Marie Veronique de Hoop Scheffer

026 **Ocean Drive** DD Allen

032 **Orange and White** Pablo Chiappori

040 **Loft within a Loft** Giovanni Longo

048 **Windmill Street** Guillaume Dreyfuss

054 **Structural Loft** Attilio Stocchi

062 **Pearl Residence** Smith & Thompson Architects

066 **Natoma Street Lofts** Jim Jennings

072 **Loft in A Coruña** A-cero

078 **House and Garage** A-cero

084 **Loft in Poblenou** Ramón Úbeda + Pepa Reverter

092 **1310 East Union** Miller/Hull Partnership

098 **Wagner Loft** Michael Carapetian

106 **Choir Loft** Delson or Sherman Architects

112 **PARTITIONS**

114 **Soho Loft** Harry Elson

120 **Park Avenue Loft** Ayhan Ozan Architects

126 **Rosenfeld Loft** Gluckman Mayner Architects

130 **Union Square Loft** James Dart

136 **Rectangular Loft** Pablo Chiaporri

142 **Decorator's Loft** Dorotea Oliva

150 **Transformable Loft** Carlo Berarducci

156 **Architect's Loft** B&B Estudio de Arquitectura, Sergi Bastidas

166 **Painter's Studio** Agnès Blanch/Elina Vila (MINIM Arquitectos)

172 **Photographer's Loft** Leddy Maytum Stacy Architects

178 **Luxurious Cell** Johnson Chou

184 **Artist's Loft** Della Valle + Bernheimer Design, Inc.

190 **INDUSTRIAL DETAILS**

192 **Stewart Loft** James Gauer

198 **Wooster Street** Lynch/Eisinger/Design

202 **Glass Bridge** David Hotson

208 **Brown Loft** Deborah Berke

214 **House and Atelier** Luis Benedit

222 **Flinders Lane** Staughton Architects

228 **Tribeca Loft** Desai/Chia Studio

232 **DISTRIBUTION and COLOR**

234 **White Loft** Anne Bugugnani and Diego Fortunato

242 **Atrium Loft** Nancy Robbins + Blau-Centre de la Llar

248 **Michigan Avenue** Pablo Uribe

256 **Flower District Loft** Desai/Chia Studio

262 **Boesky Loft** Gluckman Mayner

268 **Baron Loft** Deborah Berke

274 **All-In-One Loft** Gary Chang/EDGE (HK) Ltd.

280 **CK Loft** Lynx Architecture

288 **UNITS**

290 **Marnix Warehouse** Fokkema Architecten

298 **Flex House** Archikubik

306 **Attic in Bilbao** AV62 Arquitectos

314 **Loft in Amsterdam** Dick van Gameren (De Architectengroep)

320 **Composer's Loft** Desai/Chia Studio

326 **Pied-a-Terre** Belle van't Hoff

Today, the concept of loft living has become as much of a lifestyle choice as a fashion state-ment. Living in a loft is already a common practice among city dwellers, and has found its way into the desires of young generations in search of stylish, practical, and unconventional living spaces.

The evolution of these modernist lofts can be traced from the beginning of the loft-living rev-olution, which began in the 1950s in Manhattan, America's birthplace of the modern-day loft. At that time, artists and bohemians in search of cheap places to live and work began to move into abandoned late-nineteenth-century industrial buildings. These iron-framed buildings were once the site of garment sweatshops, furniture companies, printmaker shops, ware-houses, depositories, and factories. As industries moved away from Manhattan into cheaper areas, these buildings became vacant. Artists seized this low-cost opportunity to create a new American version of the Parisian artist's atelier and began moving into these spaces not only to work but also to live. As such, they unknowingly created what we now refer to as the *loft*.

The structural character of these buildings allowed for large, open surface areas, floor-to-ceiling windows, and an extraordinary amount of light and space. In addition to making per-fect artists' studios and galleries, they also made great homes. The early loft residents of Soho and Greenwich Village discovered that materials and objects as simple as plaster, a bookcase, or a screen could be used as partitions to divide the space. Many industrial fea-tures present in these lofts were simply retained and treated as an intrinsic characteristic of the space. Loft-style spaces soon became a mainstream way of living, as architects and developers realized how easily and affordably a loft space could be transformed into a dra-matic and alluring living unit.

Since the 1980s, the loft concept has become increasingly sophisticated, tightened its grip on countless cities in the United States, and wooed Europe and other parts of the industrialized world. Virtually any city with a stock of old industrial buildings has seen a surge of loft spaces, which has also aided in the renovation of many run-down urban areas. Consequently, people have experienced a renewed desire to live in the city, specifically in unique and innovative housing options that are available to everybody.

The contemporary notion of the loft has given way to flexible and varied interpretations of this original living space. Most loft owners are clients who buy shell spaces and have the interior professionally designed, built, and furnished. Architects who design loft conversions are particularly sensitive to the function and materials of the original building and search for a marriage between old and new that adapts to the needs and tastes of the owners. Although minimalism might still be considered the prevailing style, there is a growing diversity of loft interiors and interpretive treatments of the characteristic whitewashed walls, exposed metal, glass screens, and expansive hard floors. The loft has also become more accessible to the general public. Its original definition has been stretched and pulled to include a mass of open-plan living spaces, both old and new. Individual expression is the key; experimentation with distribution, color, texture, materials, and finishes can result in personalized spaces and urban sanctuaries in the heart of the city.

Divided into chapters on different kinds of practical solutions, this book offers a multitude of ideas on how to create a loft space in which to live and work. Whether in an industrial space or in a new construction, the feeling of a loft is always possible.

These ideas, from some of the most renowned architects in the world, can be applied to a variety of spaces and interpreted in different ways to suit personal tastes and satisfy specific requirements. More than just a fashion trend, the loft has become the expression of all things urban, the essence of contemporary living, and a peaceful and intimate retreat from a bustling metropolis.

Zartoshty Loft

Inspired by Ice

Ocean Drive

Orange and White

Loft within a Loft

Windmill Street

Structural Loft

Pearl Residence

Natoma Street Lofts

Loft in A Coruña

House and Garage

Loft in Poblenou

1310 East Union

Wagner Loft

Choir Loft

Zartoshty Loft

This loft was tailored for a bachelor who desired a space in which to **relax**, **entertain**, and host larger gatherings

Architect: **Stephen Chung**   Location: **Boston, United States**

Completion date: **2000**   Area: **2,400 sq. ft.**   Photographer: **Eric Roth**

Located on the top floor of a new artist loft building in downtown Boston, this project involved the conversion of a 2,400-square-foot raw shell into a primary residence.

At the owner's request, the architect designed a two-story living/dining area, an open kitchen, a wet bar, and a media room. A staircase, partly concealed behind a tall cupboard unit, leads to the upper mezzanine, which is designated to the master bedroom, bathroom, and study.

Zartoshty Loft

1. Living Area
2. Dining Area
3. Kitchen
4. Entertainment Room

5. Bathroom
6. Office
7. Bathroom

A limited palette of materials was used to blur the distinction between different elements and functional areas. The cabinetry, doors, trim, and most of the flooring is dark walnut wood with a matte finish, contrasted by some walls, counters, and doors that are sandblasted glass. The remaining space is rendered in veneer plaster with a semigloss surface.

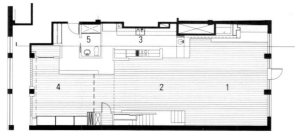

First Floor

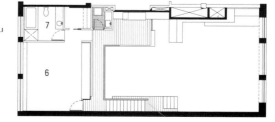

Mezzanine

Inspired by Ice

A unique interpretation of **inspired** techniques expresses a **melange** of classical, rustic, and theatrical styles

Architect: **Marie Veronique de Hoop Scheffer**   Location: **Buenos Aires, Argentina**

Completion date: **1999**   Area: **1,500 sq. ft.**   Photographer: **Virginia del Guidice**

Inspired by Ice

Occupying a former Chrysler factory, this loft was designed by Marie Veronique de Hoop Scheffer, an interior designer from Belgium. Captivated by the city of Buenos Aires and inspired by the astounding glacial landscapes of Patagonia, she discovered the Palacio Alcorta, which contains some of the most beautiful lofts in the city behind its neoclassical facade.

A grand entrance announces the way into the loft. The glacier-like platform penetrates the living area and simultaneously functions as a dining table. Its similarity to a stage creates a theatrical effect, especially at night when illuminated artificially.

The entrance platform was fashioned out of slightly polished black marble from South Africa, and the floors are a light gray wood.

The colors, mainly white, blue, and gray, were chosen by the designer for their resemblance to the glaciers of Patagonia.

White pillars punctured by glass bricks and a large gray granite platform lead down a few steps to an integrated living/dining room and kitchen.

Inspired by Ice

A staircase, designed by Marie Veronique, leads to the upper level, where a small lounge and two bedrooms are situated. Linked by a glass walkway, the two bedrooms enjoy a great deal of privacy.

A bathroom is incorporated into the main bedroom: The sinks were placed behind a counter, while the shower lies behind an opaque glass partition. The elliptical shape of the ceiling structure was preserved and emphasized by outlining the curves in blue.

Ocean Drive

The **elimination** of conventional
rooms is the first step to
achieve the true **feel** of a loft

Architect: **DD Allen**   Location: **Miami, United States**

Completion date: **1998**   Area: **624 sq. ft.**   Photographer: **Pep Escoda**

In this project, the dividing wall that previously marked off the bedroom was removed, and only the reinforced concrete column was left exposed, acting as a sculptural element in the loft.

The bed, fully integrated with the rest of the space, sits on top of a platform shaped like a grand piano and has direct views of the ocean. The column and the platform are the visual dividers between public and private space.

Designed for short stays, the kitchen was reduced to a stovetop, built-in refrigerator, and a bar that doubles as an eating table. A minimal number of elements and a light color palette create a peaceful and fresh atmosphere.

Finishes and furniture were chosen with the aim of maintaining the original character of the space. The polished concrete floor is pale turquoise, and the plaster walls are painted a lime green. The original 1960s and 1970s furniture was found at small local specialty stores.

Orange and White

Based on **simple lines** combined with the use of noble materials, this project features a **dynamic** space in which each area possesses its own characteristics

Architect: **Pablo Chiappori**   Location: **Buenos Aires, Argentina**

Completion date: **2000**   Area: **1,100 sq. ft.**   Photographer: **Virginia del Guidice**

The interaction between the proportions of the horizontal spaces and the vertical voids, as well as the amount of natural light that fills the space, are the main resources that were used to generate the individual areas of the loft.

Dark woods, natural stone, steel, and translucent fabrics in different textures are the most prominent materials.

Neutral colors with different intensities generate a tranquil environment in which special pieces stand out.

The kitchen is concealed within a module alongside the entrance hallway and incorporates a breakfast area with stools.

Among a number of artworks found inside the home, the most notable pieces include the tulip chairs by Eero Saarinen, the stools by Harry Bertoia, and the original shelf piece from the 1960s by Stilka.

Comprised of comfortable furniture and bright tones of white and orange, the living area leads to the upper level, which contains the bedroom suite.

Views between the various spaces are filtered by dividing elements, such as the large sliding wood door that constitutes one of the main decorative features of the home and disappears into the wall to permit views of the bedroom.

Orange and White

In the bedroom, a window behind the bed looks onto the lower level, and an en-suite bathroom reveals an open wash area and a more private shower and toilet.

Loft within a Loft

The architectural elements were chosen for their **contrasting volumes** in relation to their function and establish the different areas within a **fluid**, open-plan space

Architect: **Giovanni Longo**   Location: **Milan, Italy**

Completion date: **2001**   Area: **1,500 sq. ft.**   Photographer: **Andrea Martiradonna**

In what was once the site of the Schlumberger factory, this attic space was rehabilitated into a living space for a young professional. The rectangular space has a 23-foot-high ceiling. The entrance is located at one extreme, and though there is only one facade, the loft receives abundant light from a pitched glass ceiling.

The living room occupies the central area. A chimney that pierces the ceiling delineates the kitchen and dining areas, which rest underneath a lowered ceiling that stops short of either side in order to let light from the sky light pass through. The vertical void above the kitchen is intersected by a glass panel that serves as a walkway on the upper level of the attic.

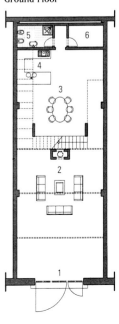

Ground Floor

Platform Floor

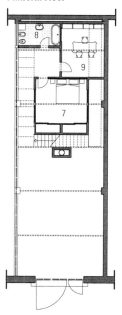

1. Entrance
2. Living Area
3. Dining Area
4. Kitchen
5. Bathroom
6. Guest room
7. Bedroom
8. Bathroom
9. Studio

A steel staircase, lightweight in comparison to the chimney, leads to the bedroom, which is sheltered inside an independent structure for ultimate privacy and an escape from daily routine. As if it were a house inside a house, as the architects refer to it, the glass catwalk that leads to the bedroom isolates it further from the surrounding area.

Sections

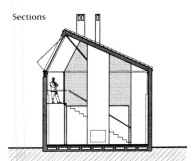

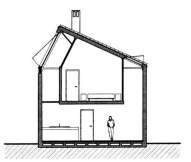

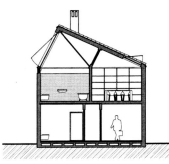

Vintage and antique furniture mingle subtly with both ordinary and designer pieces, adding a great deal of character and personality to the home. The artwork was carefully placed in relation to the surrounding features and architectural gestures.

Windmill Street

Once the sight of a **windmill** field, this nineteenth-century building was **adapted** to house a loft distributed over several levels

Architect: **Guillaume Dreyfuss**   Location: **Valletta, Malta**

Completion date: **2002**   Area: **1,600 sq. ft.**   Photographer: **Kurt Arrigo, David Pisani**

The Maltese wooden balconies that project from the facade serve as a light filter as well as a sound buffer.

The vertical shaft creates a visual link between all floors, accentuating the verticality of the house, and provides the upper levels with a heightened sensation of open space.

1. Dining Area
2. Kitchen
3. Bedrooms
4. Bathroom

Third Floor

Fourth Floor

The public zones are paved in a monolithic self-leveling concrete and resin floor and are characterized by the steel and expanded metal stairs and landings that divide the floor horizontally into two areas.

The more private bedroom area is laid with solid and resilient materials like gray terrazzo. A floor-to-ceiling closet and mosaic tile surface delineates the master bathroom.

Structural Loft

The rawness of abandoned factories demands a careful **analysis** of the space, a skillful execution of technical solutions, and an eye for transforming it into a **comfortable** living area

Architect: **Attilio Stocchi**   Location: **Bergamo, Italy**

Completion date: **2002**   Area: **1,720 sq. ft.**   Photographer: **Andrea Martiradonna**

Given the extraordinary height of the ceilings in this space, the architect decided to take advantage of the space and incorporate an additional level.

The loft is articulated through thirteen steel posts distributed in asymmetrical clusters around the space. These posts support the horizontal planes system to create the sensation of instability, piercing through what comes in their way in an arbitrary manner.

The public zone was allocated to the lower level, while the private zones were lifted onto the upper structures. Two slanted posts puncture an oval glass dining table and continue through a floating structure suspended from the ceiling that contains a bathroom.

The upper level consists of walkways flanked in glass that lead to the bathroom and bedroom. The use of glass to protect the catwalk ensures transparency and the flow of light throughout both levels of the loft. This passage not only links areas but also serves to "protect" the living area just underneath, acting as a lowered ceiling to provide a more intimate atmosphere.

Downstairs, to one side, a large stainless steel island contains the kitchen installations, except for the refrigerator, which is inserted into the back wall. The extractor pump descends from the ceiling and suspends over the stovetop.

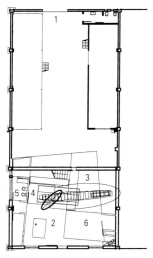

1. Entrance
2. Kitchen
3. Living Room
4. Dining Room
5. Bathroom
6. Bedroom

Floor Plan

The steel posts that culminate just behind the bed in the bedroom are both structural and decorative. Another key element is the intricate steel sculpture situated underneath a glass panel in the ground floor, which shines at night.

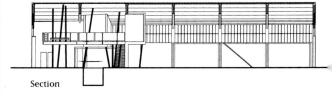

Section

Structural Loft

The strict use of steel creates a distinctive style and gives a sense of continuity within the loft.

Pearl Residence

Tall ceilings and **multifunctional**
furniture hide an endless number
of possibilities for loft-style living

Architect: **Smith & Thompson Architects**   Location: **New York City, United States**

Completion date: **2001**   Area: **1,050 sq. ft.**   Photographer: **Doug Baz**

This project was located in a converted loft building near Union Square in New York City.

The spacious living area incorporates a small mezzanine level that serves as a study and a guest room. Tall ceilings make this a comfortable space, and the use of Plexiglass on the stairs and platform lessen the obstruction of light from the large windows.

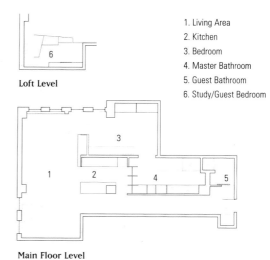

Loft Level

1. Living Area
2. Kitchen
3. Bedroom
4. Master Bathroom
5. Guest Bathroom
6. Study/Guest Bedroom

Main Floor Level

The dining table expands into the living area to accommodate 10 dinner guests.

The color palette is light, with copper highlights and metallic finishes above an ebonized wood floor.

Bathrooms were painted white to obtain a greater sense of space within rather narrow parameters.

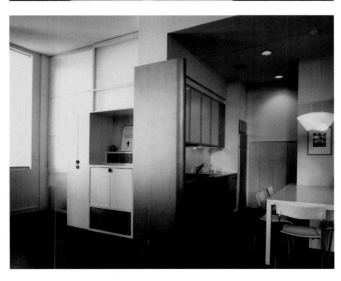

Natoma Street Lofts

The generous use of **glass** and the innovative handling of **steel** achieve a dramatic and unique collection of lofts in a small urban lot in San Francisco

Architect: **Jim Jennings**   Location: **San Francisco, United States**

Completion date: **2002**   Area: **970 sq. ft.**   Photographer: **Roger Casas**

The rectangular two-story volume led to the creation of a mezzanine level on which the bedroom is situated. A translucent glass balcony looks from the bedroom onto the living area underneath.

Steel is one of the primary resources used in this project to accomplish a modern yet raw effect throughout the loft.

Apertures were made horizontally, in the form of clerestory windows, and vertically, along a corner that is fashioned out of glass and steel, from floor to ceiling.

The dining area faces the kitchen and is separated by an island. The concrete floors and radiant heat provide an efficient means of living comfortably within this two-story space.

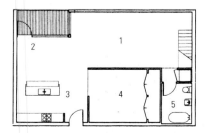

1. Living Area
2. Dining Area
3. Kitchen
4. Bedroom
5. Bathroom

Plant

Natoma Street Lofts

Loft in A Coruña

A previously dark and divided space was converted into a loft-style residence by tearing down the existing **partitions** and introducing a series of **pivoting panels**

Architect: **A-cero**   Location: **A Coruña, Spain**

Completion date: **1998**   Area: **1,020 sq. ft.**   Photographer: **Juan Rodríguez**

The existing mezzanine was preserved and modified slightly around the staircase, while eliminations were made in the hall to provide a greater sense of space in the entrance. The column that previously supported the mezzanine was replaced by a tension rod to relieve the perception of heaviness.

Stairs recessed in the wall lead to an upper level that houses the bedroom, bathroom, and dressing room.

The public areas and domestic functions are divided by small differences in levels or materials along the floor and ceiling.

A translucent glass balcony subtly divides the two levels and provides privacy for the private areas.

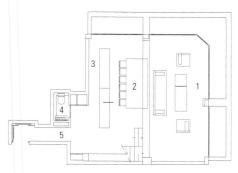

First Floor

Upper Floor

1. Living Area
2. Dining Area
3. Kitchen
4. Half-Bathroom
5. Entrance
6. Bedroom
7. Bathroom

The furnishings, from the picture frames to the armchairs, were designed as a part of the project and include a complex kitchen module that contains all the appliances and bathroom elements.

House and Garage

A former warehouse was transformed into a single, two-story space with **minimalist lines** and **strong color**

Architect: **A-cero**   Location: **A Coruña, Spain**

Completion date: **2001**   Area: **2,560 sq. ft.**   Photographer: **Alberto Peris Caminero**

Different floor levels distribute the basic functions of the loft. The lower level contains the living and dining areas. The next level, distinguished by a taller ceiling, houses an integrated kitchen that can be closed off by a sliding opaque glass panel.

The top level is accessed by a floating staircase that passes alongside a glass structure containing the main bathroom.

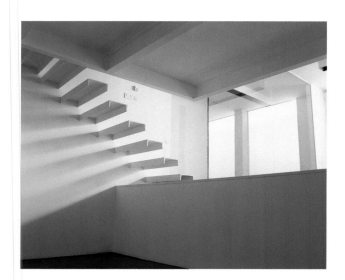

House and Garage

The decorative surprise arrives in the living area, where the family car appears behind a glass wall that corresponds to the garage. The automobile becomes an additional decorative feature of the home.

In addition to transforming an industrial space into an innovative dwelling, the purpose of this project was to explore the social significance of the automobile as a functional and aesthetic element of the home.

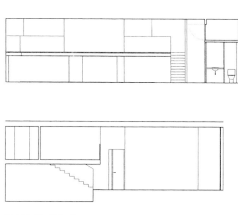

Longitudinal Sections

Glass is a crucial component of the concept and design, transforming light into an architectural element that is played with to give character to the space.

House and Garage

The other materials used, especially along the floors, also define the boundaries between areas. The lower floor is made of a red rubber surface, while the top floor was fitted out with natural coconut fiber to add warmth to the private space.

1. First Bedroom
2. Second Bedroom
3. Walk-in Closet
4. Bathroom

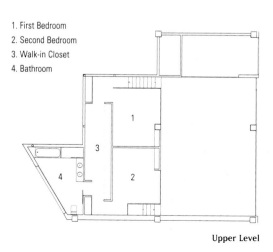

Upper Level

Loft in Poblenou

This **previously industrial** area of Barcelona houses many loft spaces that have been **renovated** and inhabited by artists and professionals

Architect: **Ramón Úbeda + Pepa Reverter**   Location: **Barcelona, Spain**

Completion date: **1998**   Area: **3,250 sq. ft.**   Photographer: **Pere Planells**

According to the architects, the existing space allowed for an easy renovation. Their aim in every residential project is to achieve spaciousness and light. The intact structure offered more than 3,000 square feet of clear and open space that most conventional spaces do not enjoy.

Massive windows occupy the perimeter of the loft, flooding the interior with natural light. A continuous resin pavement covers the floors, bouncing the light up into every corner.

A staircase leads to the mezzanine level, which houses a den and an artist's workshop.

Loft in Poblenou

The wood floor on the upper level incorporates a series of glass inserts with built-in lights that illuminate from the floor up.

The living and dining areas occupy the main space, dominated by a vast wall of windows. The decoration, infused by its creators and tenants, is minimalist and colorful, with certain modernist touches.

The mixture of styles can be seen in the bathrooms, for example, in which one is more minimalist, using wood and translucent glass, and the other is more personalized, with an amusing tile pattern imitated by the piles of books on the floor.

1310 East Union

The building is a structural type of architecture that conveys a sense of economy, **efficiency**, discipline, and **order**, all of which are essential characteristics of urban loft living

Architect: **Miller/Hull Partnership**   Location: **Seattle, United States**

Completion date: **2002**   Area: **700 to 1,600 sq. ft.**   Photographers: **Ben Benschneider, James F. Housel, Craig Richmond**

Located on Capitol Hill in Seattle, Washington, this loft-style condominium project occupies a small 40 by 80 plot that was maximized by the architects' design plan. Each residential floor contains two loft units varying in size from 700 to 1,600 square feet.

The top two floors contain duplexes, one of which is shown here, with west-facing balconies, mezzanines, and shared access to a private rooftop garden.

The duplex contains integrated living/dining/kitchen areas on the lower level, which look out through a steel-framed glass facade with uninterrupted views of the city.

Interior materials include concrete floors, exposed steel structural elements, steel railings, steel-plate baseboards, and modular metal kitchen casework supporting the butcher-block counters. Patches of color liven up the space.

The kitchen was placed along the back wall so that the living and dining areas
could take most advantage of the natural light and vistas.

1. Living Area
2. Kitchen
3. Bathroom

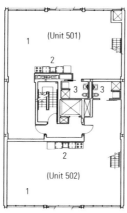

Fifth Floor

1. Void
2. Bedroom
3. Bathroom

Fifth Floor Mezzanine

The mezzanine on the upper level houses the bedroom and, like the lower level, has access to the private rooftop terrace.

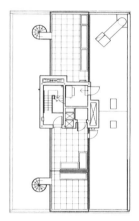

Roof Terrace

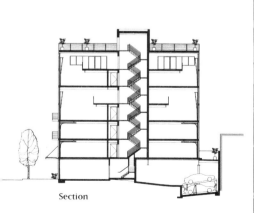

Section

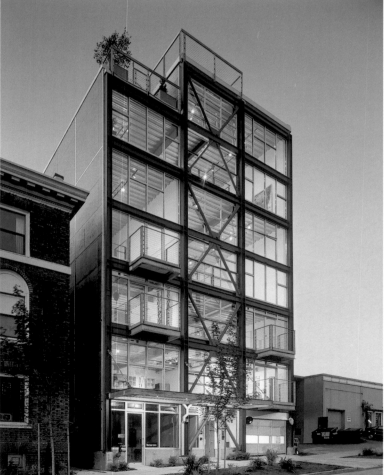

Wagner Loft

The wish to keep separate the new intervention from the **historical fabric** of the industrial shell was the **driving concept** behind Michael Carapetian's design

Architect: **Michael Carapetian**   Location: **Venice, Italy**

Completion date: **1998**   Area: **3,200 sq. ft.**   Photographer: **Andrea Martiradonna**

The residence was inserted into an industrial shell that was originally constructed in 1910 and known as the Dreher Brewery. The aim of the architect was to keep the structure intact by introducing new surfaces to sustain the rooms without removing any of the existing brick walls and wood trusses.

Wagner Loft

The terraces and the lowest level of the loft are raised by a suspended steel floor and a suspended steel-frame wall that divides the space from the rest of the enveloping structure. An elliptical-shaped wood construction is cantilevered from two wood structural plates, taking up one-third of the space. This ellipse, which makes reference to conventional boat constructions, is composed of prefabricated plywood box-beams.

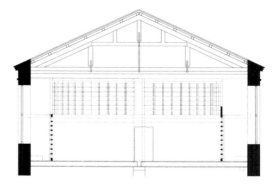

Section

A glass and stainless steel staircase guides the circulation throughout the space and terminates in the sleeping gallery, which holds a suspended circular bathtub and a glass bathroom.

1. Kitchen
2. Dining Area
3. Bedroom
4. Bathroom
5. Living Room Area
6. Bedroom
7. Bathroom

Level 1

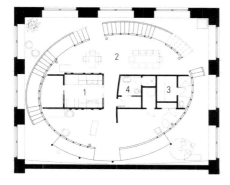

Level 2

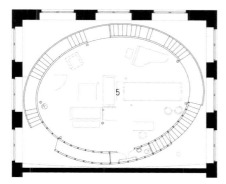

Level 3

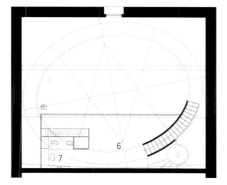

The wooden deck consists of paths and small ponds of water, an ideal place to relax and enjoy the views of distant Venice.

Choir Loft

Harboring a **volume of light** and space, this loft preserves the **high ceilings** and wooden structure that was previously the site of a milk-distribution warehouse in the early 1900s

Architect: **Delson or Sherman Architects**   Location: **Brooklyn, United States**

Completion date: **2002**   Area: **1,400 sq. ft.**   Photographer: **Catherine Tighe**

In order to emphasize the vastness of the two-story volume, a series of deep skylights that spill light into the space was installed into the ceiling. The room was furnished with a giant 20-foot table and long bookcases.

The warehouse was converted into a church decades later, in the 1930s. Architects bought the neglected property and transformed it into a home for a family of four. The space was gutted out, although even the shell was in need of repair. Major structural work included rebuilding an exterior wall and bolstering existing trusses with new heavy-timber struts and steel plates.

The industrial character of the space was maintained, leaving the new masonry wall exposed and painting the stripped floors.

The mezzanine, which previously was the church's choir loft, contains an intimate living area and shelters another sitting area underneath, offering cozy alternatives to the big room.

Choir Loft

A stainless steel kitchen is a welcome contrast to the wood framework of the loft.

The renovations were inspired by minimalist 1970s architecture, the building itself conveying a rough-hewn feel that is distinctly modern.

Mezzanine

1. Sitting Room
2. Bedrooms
3. Bathroom
4. Guestroom

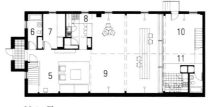

Main Floor

5. Living Room
6. Bathroom
7. Office
8. Kitchen
9. Dining Area
10. Guest Living Room
11. Guest Kitchen

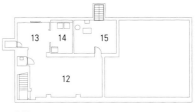

Cellar

12. Studio
13. Storage
15. Laundry
15. Boiler Room

Soho Loft

Park Avenue Loft

Rosenfeld Loft

Union Square Loft

Rectangular Loft

Decorator's Loft

Transformable Loft

Architect's Loft

Painter's Studio

Photographer's Loft

Luxurious Cell

Artist's Loft

Soho Loft

The architect's intention was to create a **dynamic** space that defined the loft experience but at the same time inject it with a more **serene** attitude

Architect: **Harry Elson**   Location: **New York City, United States**

Completion date: **2002**   Area: **1,000 sq. ft.**   Photographer: **Paul Warchol**

The existing space, with 14-foot ceilings and floor-to-ceiling windows, had been previously subdivided into small rooms. In order to reclaim the length and height of the space, a single 10-foot-high and 30-inch-thick floating wall was constructed to divide the space into two distinct zones: the public living area and the semiprivate bedroom area.

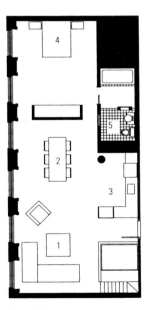

Floor Plan

1. Living Area
2. Dining Area
3. Kitchen
4. Bedroom
5. Bathroom

A cubelike sleeping loft, placed in the corner of the space in alignment with the end of the kitchen cabinetry and bathroom wall, incorporates a coat closet on the entry side and a media cabinet on the living area side.

To enhance the fluid relationship between the various spaces, the client requested a custom bed and side tables to match the pieces purchased for the dining and living areas. Furthermore, the sofa and dining table chairs were finished in the same color to create a visual link between the two areas.

The L-shaped maple kitchen cabinetry, which contrasts with the dark-stained existing floor, visually separates the living area from the dining area and physically separates the kitchen from the entrance. The only door in the loft is a 10-foot-high pocket door that leads to the private bathroom area.

Park Avenue Loft

To construct this loft, the best option was to gut the interior and start from **scratch**, using the **raw open** space as the starting point for the renovation

Architect: **Ayhan Ozan Architects**   Location: **New York City, United States**

Completion date: **2000**   Area: **2,500 sq. ft.**   Photographer: **Bjorg Photography**

Acid-etched glass, the most important material present, was used to create divisions that optimize the circulation of light.

The concept was developed around an open, sky-lit kitchen designed as a freestanding island within the living area to enhance the feeling of spaciousness.

A second design element was to allow daylight to penetrate all areas of the loft. To achieve this, no single wall reaches the ceiling, and a select few are surrounded by glass. The two large walls at either end of the living room, framed from behind by acid-etched glass panels, mark the passageway into the private areas and act as an attractive backdrop for paintings and other objects.

Park Avenue Loft

Cabinets were integrated within the perimeter windowsills to provide extra storage, and their wide surface also doubles as additional seating during parties and gatherings.

In this case, the previously existing sprinkler pipes were hidden from view to keep the ceilings clean and uninterrupted.

Floor Plan

1. Living/Dining Area
2. Kitchen
3. Gallery
4. Master Bedroom
5. Master Bathroom
6. Hallway
7. Exercise Room
8. Bathroom
9. Bedrooms

An elaborate lighting system offers different lighting schemes to achieve a variety of moods. All bathroom fixtures are by Philippe Stark.

Rosenfeld Loft

The rough qualities of a warehouse
were **polished** and **enhanced**
by fine architectural detailing in
this 4,000-square-foot space

Architect: **Gluckman Mayner Architects**   Location: **New York City, United States**

Completion date: **1998**   Area: **4,000 sq. ft.**   Photographer: **Lydia Gould Bessler**

This residence includes a 1,800-square-foot living space, two bedrooms, an open kitchen, and a 400-square-foot outdoor terrace.

The finishes are refined: The original vaulted ceiling was subtly altered to achieve a smooth, curvy effect, and the brick walls and pillars were painted white to maintain a sober color palette.

A delicate arch leads the way into one of the bedrooms, draped with translucent fabrics that soften the linear aspect of the loft.

A partition runs the length of the dining area to give privacy to the living areas, incorporating a small aquarium that also acts as a window between the two spaces.

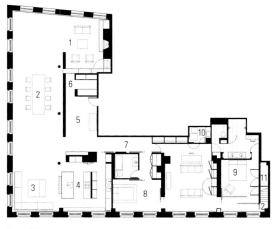

Floor Plan

1. Living Area
2. Dining Area
3. Lounge
4. Kitchen
5. Entry
6. Closet
7. Corridor
8. Bedroom
9. Master Bedroom
10. Study
11. Closet
12. Utility

A steel-framed sliding door opens to reveal the second bedroom. The minimal detailing and strict use of color is consistent throughout the entire residence.

Union Square Loft

Just off of Union Square in New York City, this loft apartment is characterized primarily by its **panoramic views** of the **urban** landscape

Architect: **James Dart**   Location: **New York City, United States**

Completion date: **2001**   Area: **1,500 sq. ft.**   Photographer: **Catherine Tighe**

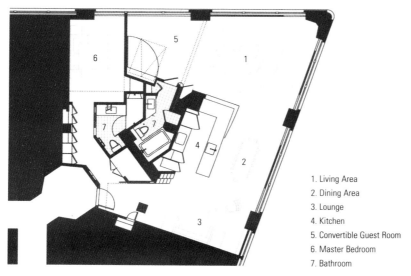

Floor Plan

1. Living Area
2. Dining Area
3. Lounge
4. Kitchen
5. Convertible Guest Room
6. Master Bedroom
7. Bathroom

A small reading area behind the living room can be transformed into a guest bedroom by pulling out the floor-to-ceiling sliding panels and convertible bed hidden inside the wall.

Union Square Loft

Occupying the oblique corner of 4th Avenue and 12th Street, architects sought to play off of the irregular geometry of the plan to create a series of framed views of the city.

The decoration is restrained, though not minimalist, and favors the use of symmetry and neutral colors.

The new design incorporates a central core composed of the kitchen and bathroom, so as to provide uninterrupted views of the exterior through the perimeter windows. The stairs along the side leads to the mezzanine level, which houses a small library and the master bedroom beyond.

Rectangular Loft

Steel columns, a vaulted ceiling
and **large** windows are a constant
reminder of the loft's original function

Architect: **Pablo Chiaporri**   Location: **Buenos Aires, Argentina**

Completion date: **1999**   Area: **1,500 sq. ft.**   Photographer: **Virginia del Guidice**

This loft is situated inside a building that was once part of the Molinos Minetti warehouses in Buenos Aires. Characterized by contemporary lines and its careful selection of furniture and objects, the space follows a simple L-shaped plan in which public and private is divided by the use of a full-length translucent fabric.

A curved staircase leads to a guest bedroom upstairs.

White and dark wood compose the color scheme of the space, and contemporary objects are interspersed with furniture from the 1940's and 50's. Designer pieces combine with objects that the architect has collected over time which reveal his personality.

Underneath this staircase, the kitchen is integrated across from the living room, behind a partition laminated in Caoba wood. White and dark wood compose the color scheme of the space, while the steel columns, vaulted ceiling, and large windows are a constant reminder of the loft's original purpose.

Rectangular Loft

The verticality of the drapes, which conceal the bedroom, emphasizes the height of the ceiling, and their translucency adds an intimate and lightweight quality to the bedroom.

Decorator's Loft

The purpose behind Dorotea Oliva's design was based on the **freedom** of space, the lack of boundaries, intimacy, **purity**, and peace

Interior designer: **Dorotea Oliva**　　　Location: **Buenos Aires, Argentina**

Completion date: **2000**　　Area: **850 sq. ft.**　　Photographer: **Virginia del Guidice**

Volume, space, and natural light conform to the necessary functional requirements so that the home is both aesthetically pleasing and practical.

In avoiding any structural walls or tall partitions, the space was divided by a half-height, 5-foot module that serves two functions.

The side facing the bed holds aluminum shelves for the entertainment equipment, while the other side is a library that incorporates two extendable light fixtures that shed light on the antique desk.

The bathroom is contained within a canopy-like structure consisting of white walls and a rotating mirror designed by Dorotea Oliva to provide versatility.

Inside is a black marble granite surface with rectangular washbasins. The toilet was placed separately behind a door to maintain privacy.

The adjacent wall was taken advantage of by placing shelves for towels and toiletries as well as another antique chest of drawers. The colors used, mainly white, turquoise, and black, optimize the fluidity of light and the overall feeling of continuity and peace.

Decorator's Loft

The opaque glass closet doors and panel behind the bed provide a soothing background, and multicolored glass shelves refract colorful rays of light that come in through the large windows.

Transformable Loft

An apartment can be **transformed**
into a loft through the removal of walls
and the insertion of **sliding panels**

Architect: **Carlo Berarducci**   Location: **Rome, Italy**

Completion date: **2001**   Area: **1,600 sq. ft.**   Photographer: **Roberto Pierucci**

This loft consists of two areas: a large rectangular space flanked by a wall of windows and another with glass doors that open onto a private terrace. These areas are divided by a sequence of pillars and sliding panels.

Two large sliding panels screen off the living and dining areas from the entrance, while a set of hinged panels fold out to close off one area so that it may be used as a guest bedroom. These folding panels reduce to the width of the pillar, leaving the living space completely open.

A suspended blue wall and a stone platform into which the mattress is inserted delineate the bedroom.

Floor Plan

1. Living Area
2. Dining Area
3. Kitchen
4. Bathrooms
5. Bedroom

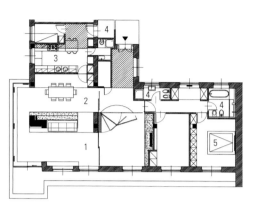

In the kitchen, the black granite countertop extends beyond the kitchen module to serve as a bar or breakfast table. In the bathroom, the same intense blue that was used as a backdrop to the bedroom covers the floors.

Architect's Loft

The **solutions** adopted to convert this industrial space into a home office atmosphere were **subtle** and based on a careful distribution of space

Architect: **B&B Estudio de Arquitectura, Sergi Bastidas**   Location: **Mallorca, Spain**

Completion date: **1999**   Area: **3,230 sq. ft.**   Photographer: **Pere Planells**

This preexisting warehouse in Mallorca preserves its industrial character in terms of both the exterior and the interior.

The first step was the creation of large, finely framed glass panels to separate the building entrance from the vestibule, revealing views of the impressive interior from outside the building. Once inside, large half-height partitions were employed to differentiate areas and to emphasize the dimensions of the loft.

A concrete staircase leads upstairs to a studio and meeting room, separated by sliding partitions. The pitched ceiling always remains exposed. Rugs were put down to lend a more personalized atmosphere.

Another partition, flanked by two columns, divides the office and the kitchen. From here, one can appreciate the encompassing structure of the loft.

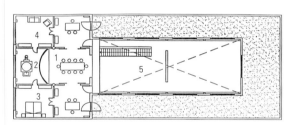

Upper Floor

Lower Floor

1. Meeting Room
2. Bathroom
3. Bedroom
4. Living Area
5. Void
6. Garage
7. Entry
8. Studio
9. Bathroom
10. Office

Architect's Loft

A recent addition to the top floor includes kitchen/dining areas, a living room, and a bedroom.

The new living area is wrapped in metal siding and adorned with a bright red leather sofa.

The all-white bedroom creates an attractive
color contrast and a light, heavenly feel.

Painter's Studio

A **single** space should be filled with light, color, and objects that contribute to a **harmonious** atmosphere

Architect: **Agnès Blanch/Elina Vila (MINIM Arquitectos)**   Location: **Barcelona, Spain**

Completion date: **2002**   Area: **1,000 sq. ft.**   Photographer: **Jose Luis Hausmann**

The loft was created for a multimedia artist whose colorful works add life to the space.

Painter's Studio

The philosophy of these interior designers springs from the perception of minimalism as a series of concepts that value simplicity, austerity, and elegance, rather than a passing aesthetic trend.

The kitchen became the center of attention; a freestanding island with a stainless steel countertop faces the living area, flanked by a wall of cabinetry.

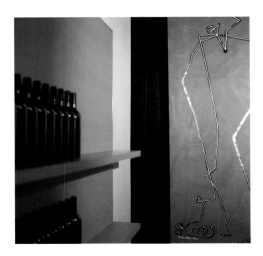

A partition conceals the bedroom and stops short of the ceiling to favor the entry of light.

In the bedroom, an original sculpture piece serves as a decorative and practical coat hanger.

The bathroom is situated behind a half-height stone wall, preserving the view of the tall windows and the structural columns. In contrast to these solid structures, light materials, such as wood and glass, were used to design the bathroom. The counter seems to float between the two columns, while the glass basin rests lightly on top of it.

Photographer's Loft

This photographer's loft is an **expansion**
of a former paint factory, transformed into a
photography studio and residence with
spectacular views of the San Francisco Bay

Architect: **Leddy Maytum Stacy Architects**   Location: **San Francisco, United States**

Completion date: **1997**   Area: **755 sq. ft.**   Photographer: **Stan Musilek, Sharon Reisdorph**

The apartment is laid out in a series of consecutive spaces. The studio is located on the ground floor, followed by a mezzanine and the upper floor, where the living space is located and where the roof serves as an outdoor terrace.

The service area, composed of the kitchen, bathroom, and storage, is separated by a staircase from the main living space, which contains the bedroom, dining room, and living room. Here, the panoramic views dominate the interior.

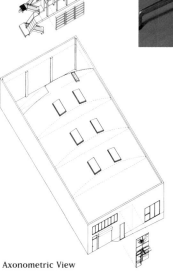

Axonometric View

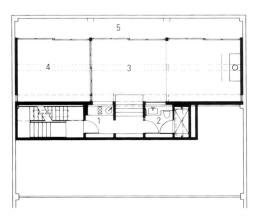

1. Entry/kitchen
2. Bathroom
3. Living/Dining
4. Bedroom
5. Terrace

Floor Plan

The living areas contain no divisions except for a sliding glass door that partitions off the bedroom. Huge windows integrate the interior with the exterior views.

Photographer's Loft

The kitchen and bathroom are situated on a level slightly below the main space,
yet also maintain a generous view of the bay.

Luxurious Cell

In renovating this loft the architect
drew on the common notions of a
prison cell: raw material, **surveillance**,
and the **absence** of excess

Architect: **Johnson Chou**   Location: **Toronto, Canada**

Completion date: **2001**   Area: **1,000 sq. ft.**   Photographer: **Volker Seding Photography**

The architect began by removing all non-structural walls and introducing a large 30-foot sandblasted screen to divide the main space. In addition, he layered the space with sliding partitions, the largest a dramatic 16-foot section of stainless steel that separates the bedroom from the living area.

In the bedroom, an aluminum-clad king-size bed cantilevered from the wall floats before a wall of floor-to-ceiling aluminum closets that span the length of the room.

The platform on which the bathing areas are located are clad in blue-green slate and distinguished by a sculptural, free-standing stainless steel vanity that heralds the passage into the washing areas. A massive white column contrasts the smoothness of the steel and glass, whose constant presence lend a certain depth and warmth despite their cool and bare qualities.

1. Entry
2. Living/Dining
3. Kitchen
4. Bedroom
5. Bathroom

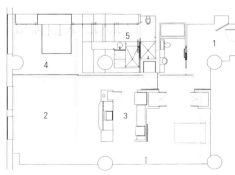

Floor Plan

A 10-inch strip of clear glass along the bathroom door indulges the voyeur with a panoramic view of the sunken slate bathtub from the living area.

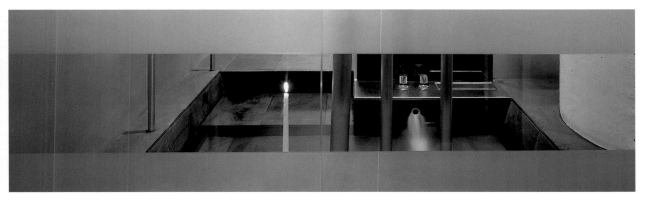

Artist's Loft

The application of **new technologies** assisted in the creation of steel **curvilinear** walls in this artist's loft in Brooklyn, New York

Architect: **Della Valle + Bernheimer Design, Inc.**   Location: **Brooklyn, United States**

Completion date: **2000**   Area: **2,500 sq. ft.**   Photographer: **Richard Barnes**

The project was designed for a ceramist/painter and her husband, an inventor and computer scientist. The implementation of steel provided a neutral yet rich backdrop for the artist's work as well as a futuristic and modern one in relation to the husband's work.

The client demanded three distinct types of spaces—private/domestic, public/studio, and private/studio.

Floor Plan

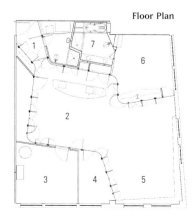

1. Entrance
2. Living Area/Kitchen
3. Ceramics Studio
4. Office
5. Painting Studio
6. Master Bedroom
7. Master Bathroom

The northernmost line segregates the private area of the loft, which contains the master bedroom and the bathrooms. The southernmost line segregates the private studio, which includes the ceramics studio and meditation space. The remaining area of the apartment, between these two curved walls, is a kitchen and painting studio. This open space becomes a gallery at intermittent times during the year for public viewing sessions.

The two walls are fabricated from laser-cut steel. These metal panels are punctuated by perforations that are meant for door pulls and hooks on which to hang the artist's work. The laser-cutting technology offered an economically efficient and technically accurate process. To fabricate the panels, computerized architectural drawings were submitted digitally to the laser-cutter and input directly into the machinery. Thus, there was no discrepancy between the preliminary drawing and the final product.

In order to attain spatial fluidity and efficiency, a hinging system was designed along the walls so that nearly all the panels pivot as conventional closet or pantry doors.

Stewart Loft
Wooster Street
Glass Bridge
Brown Loft
House and Atelier
Flinders Lane
Tribeca Loft

Stewart Loft

A **generously** windowed **rectangular**
space was fitted out for living and
dining areas, a kitchen island,
and an imposing grand piano

Architect: **James Gauer**   Location: **New York City, United States**

Completion date: **2001**   Area: **2,200 sq. ft.**   Photographer: **Catherine Tighe**

This 2,200-square-foot loft is located at the edge of Manhattan's flower district. In its original state, it boasted oversized industrial steel sash windows on one side and two full-height windows on the other, providing architects with a fundamental element with which to work.

A perimeter of private space and a core of service areas were created, differentiated from one another by the materials chosen to reinforce each.

Floor Plan

1. Entrance
2. Living Area
3. Dining Area
4. Kitchen
5. Master Bedroom
6. Master Bathroom
7. Guest Bedroom/Study

Thick storage walls separate the perimeter rooms, which are covered in silver dusted brown paper and flanked by translucent glass doors in aluminum frames.

Lighting was also used to reinforce the distinction between the core and the perimeter. A small recessed fixture lights the core, and a cable system suspended below the exposed ceiling beams and sprinkler pipes underscores the linear nature of the perimeter spaces.

The master suite and study/guest room are situated at the far end of the loft beyond the translucent glass doors.

The core was sheathed in maple panels, and the perimeter walls and ceilings were painted white over plaster. Stainless steel punctuates the core at the entry door and kitchen counter. The perimeter floor was laid in maple, while floors in the core are limestone.

Furnishings are deliberately spare; most are designer pieces, and the grand piano is a black Steinway.

The architect designed the maple bed and headboard panel in the master suite.
A translucent glass door allows light into the master bathroom.

Wooster Street

Inspired by the original Soho
artists' lofts of the **1970s**, this loft
bases its design on the **raw** qualities
inherent to previously industrial spaces

Architect: **Lynch/Eisinger/Design**   Location: **New York City, United States**

Completion date: **2002**   Area: **1,500 sq. ft.**   Photographer: **Albert Vecerka**

Unlike many lofts today, in which the spaces are divided and decorated beyond recognition, this one treats its transformation into a living space as a "building-within-a-site" rather than an adding onto or complete conversion of the space.

The architects' approach was to clear away all existing partitions and concentrate the new construction—kitchen, bath, bedroom, and dressing room—along a single wall. The new elements are treated as an insertion of cabinetry into and distinct from the enclosing volume.

The existing iron columns were stripped and restored to contrast the white walls and light wood floors.

Humble materials, like birch, plywood, and acrylic, were used to highlight the original character of the space. Walls and ceilings were restored with smooth white plaster and contrast the new wood cabinetry, which blends into the restored maple floors.

Wooster Street

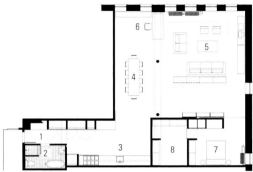

Floor Plan

1. Entrance
2. Bathroom
3. Kitchen
4. Dining Area
5. Living Area
6. Study
7. Bedroom
8. Dressing Room

The bedroom lies behind an 8-foot by 8-foot door, composed of acrylic on a wood frame, which slides away into the cabinet wall that separates this area from the living room and kitchen.

Glass Bridge

A gut renovation led to
the creation of a generous, **two-story**
space designed to **adapt** to a
young couple with children

Architect: **David Hotson**   Location: **New York City, United States**

Completion date: **2000**   Area: **2,500 sq. ft.**   Photographer: **Eduard Hueber**

The project is rendered as a series of clearly defined interacting volumes. The principal volume of the two-story living area is delineated by full-height walls on three sides and carried across the fourth side by the glass and aluminum mezzanine railings and the overhanging upper-level bedroom.

The kitchen and dining area, media room and bridge are configured as secondary volumes sheathed in translucent glass.

At the mezzanine level, the floor joining the media room with the children's bedrooms was constructed of laminated glass and configured as a bridge passing over the dining area.

To allow light into the private areas, the partitions that separate these rooms were fashioned from etched glass panels framed in aluminum and composed of hinged leaves, which allow the rooms to join the living space.

Materials are treated as the surfaces of concave spaces, thus treating the volume as an architectural space rather than a sculptural form.

Upper Level

Lower Level

1. Entry
2. Living Area
3. Dining Area
4. Kitchen
5. Service Entrance
6. Master Bedroom
7. Master Bathroom
8. Dressing Area
9. Stair
10. Media Room
11. Glass Bridge
12. Bedroom
13. Bathroom

Brown Loft

An emphasis on **perspective**, an open plan, and a muted palette of materials afford a sense of **spaciousness** and light to this Soho loft

Architect: **Deborah Berke**   Location: **New York City, United States**

Completion date: **1999**   Area: **3,700 sq. ft.**   Photographer: **Catherine Tighe**

Part of a renovated industrial building, this space was fitted out for an artist and illustrator who wanted a space for living, working, and entertaining clients.

The original columns of the building were left retained and restored, acting as a polished foil for the modernity of the renovation. Their presence creates an invisible line between the kitchen and living areas.
Translucent acrylic and aluminum partitions allow for flexible divisions between the major spaces and disappear discreetly into pockets in the wall.

Brown Loft

1. Foyer
2. Living Area
3. Dining Area
4. Kitchen
5. Pantry
6. Bathroom
7. Study
8. Media Room
9. Dressing Room
10. Guest Bathroom
11. Guest Bedroom
12. Master Bedroom
13. Dressing Room
14. Laundry
15. Storage

Floor Plan

Industrial attributes, such as the sprinkler pipes along the ceiling, were restored and kept exposed as a reminder of the building's original state.

A kitchen island is always useful in an open-plan space, acting simultaneously as a working surface, eating table, and divider between kitchen and living areas.

House and Atelier

Versatility and **character** define
this spacious loft, adaptable to
the constant movement and daily
lifestyle of an artist/architect

Architect: **Luis Benedit**   Location: **Buenos Aires, Argentina**

Completion date: **1999**   Area: **1,830 sq. ft.**   Photographer: **Virginia del Guidice**

This loft was previously a bakery shop that was part of an old market. It belongs to Luis Benedit, a well-known artist and architect who has exhibited his work in the New York Museum of Modern Art and the Contemporary Art Museum in Sydney, Australia. He decided to buy the 1,830 square-foot space and transform it into his own living and working space.

To create a more homely atmosphere, the owner coated the walls with panels of Guatambú wood. He also introduced a quartz lighting system along the industrial ceiling grill.

The public areas were distributed along the 130-foot long loft.

The kitchen and living area share an elevated surface to differentiate them from the remaining studio space. The use of different levels is a valuable technique for small or narrow spaces in order to create different environments.

A few designer pieces, such as the office chair and red sofa, add a contemporary air to the hand-made space.

The kitchen can be seen through a dilapidated wall on the far end, which was left intact, and the countertop was made from tiles (in two colors) that were found at a demolition site.

The bedroom features a chair designed by Benedit, an art-deco night table, and a painting by Pat Andrea.

House and Atelier

The bathroom was also fashioned out of recycled objects, such as the tiles, the large washbasin, and the shelves made out of pieces of tree trunk.

Flinders Lane

Located in the heart of Melbourne, Australia, this **industrial** space fitted out as a residence boasts a raw shell of pipes, **concrete**, and tall windows

Architect: **Staughton Architects**   Location: **Melbourne, Australia**

Completion date: **2000**   Area: **850 sq. ft.**   Photographer: **Shannon Mcrath**

The project is defined by two principal elements. The first is a multifunctional, freestanding wood-framed unit that encloses the sleeping area, provides storage space, serves as an auxiliary dining room, includes bookshelves, and is a sculptural element by itself. The second element is the set of patterns sandblasted into the original cement floor.

The industrial character of the space was preserved by retaining features such as the original ventilation ducts, wrought-iron piping, and original concrete floors.

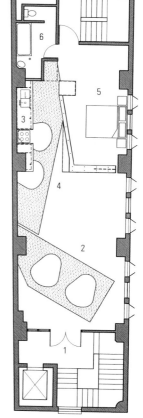

1. Entry
2. Living Area
3. Kitchen
4. Dining Area
5. Bedroom
6. Bathroom

Floor Plan

The bedroom unit is independent, touching neither the ceiling nor the lateral walls, and could be easily mistaken for a piece of furniture.

While the wood and polycarbonate unit separates the space into bedroom and living room, it also delimits the kitchen and guides traffic to the narrow entrance of the bedroom and bathroom.

Flinders Lane

In addition to performing multiple functions, the polycarbonate and wood unit also acts as a lamp against which shadows become visible.

Tribeca Loft

This Tribeca loft consists of a
large **open** floor plan that uses
the minimum number of walls to create
a sequence of **luminous** spaces

Architect: **Desai/Chia Studio**   Location: **New York City, United States**

Completion date: **1998**   Area: **5,000 sq. ft.**   Photographer: **Joshua McHugh**

A new floating ceiling was "cut and folded," creating sloped coves that bounce incandescent light down into the space. These coves define seating, dining, and sleeping areas.

Only the bedroom and bathrooms have doors for privacy, while the remaining spaces—the library, kitchen, living area, and dining area—are screened from each other by carefully deployed partitions. The slits in between these partitions play a visual game of implied and real translucency, providing glimpses into and emitting light from the spaces within.

The dining table and columns, fashioned out of the same material, establish a polished and coherent aspect in this sculptural space.

Floor Plan

1. Entry
2. Dining Area
3. Living Area
4. Kitchen
5. Library
6. Guest Bathroom
7. Master Bathroom
8. Dressing Area
9. Master Bedroom
10. Mechanical Room

A tight palette of raw materials, mainly concrete, wood, glass, and steel, are applied to grant a tactile nature that balances texture, scale, and color.

White Loft
Atrium Loft
Michigan Avenue
Flower District Loft
Boesky Loft
Baron Loft
All-In-One Loft
CK Loft

White Loft

A former studio within an industrial building was transformed into a white **haven** that reconciles the qualities of its noisy neighborhood with its **peaceful** landscaped terrace

Architect: **Anne Bugugnani and Diego Fortunato**   Location: **Barcelona, Spain**

Completion date: **2000**   Area: **1,400 sq. ft.**   Photographer: **Eugeni Pons**

The concept revolved around the marriage between contrasting elements: the visually chaotic interior patio and the mathematic collection of volumes, the cool metallic emergency stairwell, and the soft white stucco that enfolds the loft.

The design focused on the essential functions, always optimizing the versatility of an open space and the entry of natural light.

The square space was sustained by a central column and a transver which act as invisible boundaries between public and private areas. tions are characterized by freestanding structural elements, such as t define the kitchen, wardrobe, and bathroom.

The partition that encloses the wardrobe features a narrow slit that maintains visual fluidity between spaces.

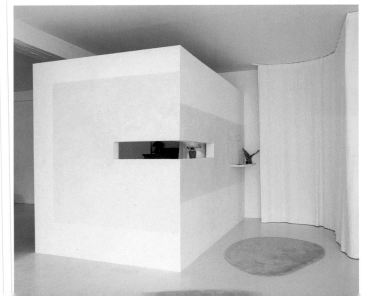

White Loft

A corner is equipped with a multitude of shelves
to provide a practical workshop area.

The open-plan bathroom creates a private corner
to which the bedroom was allocated.

1. Entry
2. Office
3. Living Area
4. Kitchen
5. Wardrobe
6. Bathroom
7. Bedroom

Floor Plan

Atrium Loft

A small space was converted
into a loft-style residence through
the **varied** use of materials, lighting,
and practical **distribution**

Architect: **Nancy Robbins + Blau-Centre de la Llar**   Location: **Barcelona, Spain**

Completion date: **2002**   Area: **900 sq. ft.**   Photographer: **Jose Luis Hausmann**

The public and private zones of this loft revolve around a glass atrium. This structure creates a U-shaped plan in which to incorporate a living area, kitchen/dining areas, a bedroom, and a bathroom.

The kitchen has a translucent white curtain that can be drawn to conceal it from the living room, when desired.

Given the narrow area designated to the kitchen and dining areas, the stainless steel island was simply extended for use as a dining table. The island makes room for mobile storage units underneath the service area, and a raised level on the floor indicates the eating area. A skylight just above the dining area was draped with a white fabric to diffuse the natural light.

The bedroom was placed on the other side of the atrium, farthest from the day area. The lighting plays an important role in setting a serene mood, both in the bedroom and bathroom.

The en-suite bathroom is wrapped in translucent glass and features an integrated shower on a wooden deck surface.

Michigan Avenue

The lack of abundant space need
not be an impediment to creating
a loft; **practical** features and
multifunctional furniture are key

Architect: **Pablo Uribe**   Location: **Miami, United States**

Completion date: **2000**   Area: **485 sq. ft.**   Photographer: **Pep Escoda**

The bedroom and living room are one shared space—the outer rim and armrests of the bed structure allow for a place to sit, and the addition of pillows creates a sofa effect.

The original wood floor was painted white to create a contemporary atmosphere and a seamless effect between wall and floor, thus making the space look larger. The bathroom is accessed by a corridor and is the only space hidden from sight. Here, a 22-foot-long towel rack offers a place to dry towels and swimsuits, reflecting the beach atmosphere that is so important to this city.

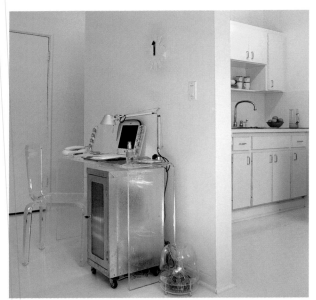

A small office area was placed in front of the bed/sofa, employing light and transparent materials to avoid any perception of bulk or heaviness.

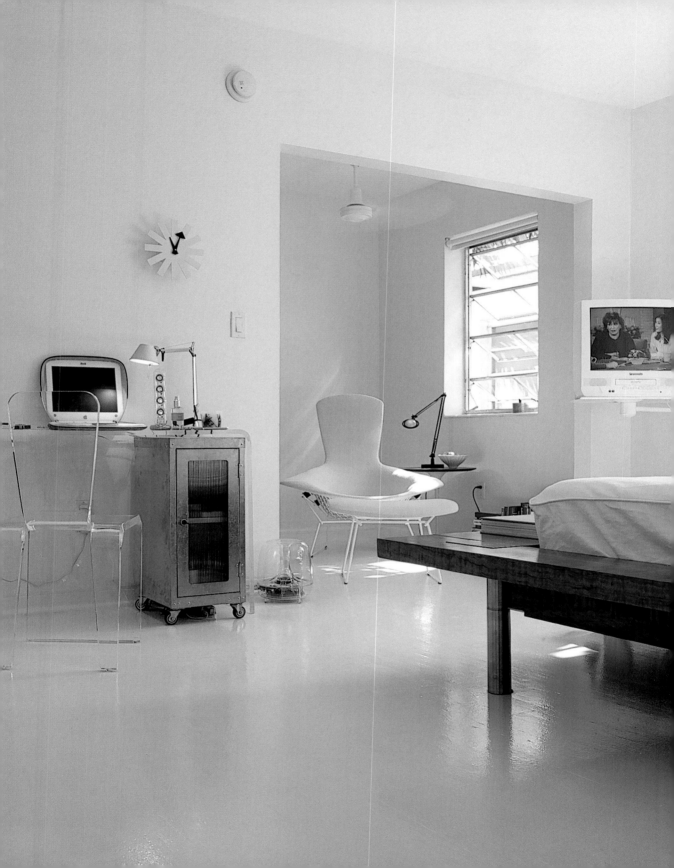

The furniture was chosen to make the best out of the limited space, creating a series of multifunctional areas. Designer chairs are a decorative means of offering a place for guests. A small reading area was situated next to the window as an extension to the living area.

Michigan Avenue

The kitchen remains out of sight from the entrance and is delineated by a portico, which provides a feeling of separation. It is also painted in white and features a compact refrigerator on wheels that can be easily moved.

Flower District Loft

The client wished for design that
would accommodate office work
by day and large business events or
intimate social gatherings **by night**

Architect: **Desai/Chia Studio**   Location: **New York City, United States**

Completion date: **2002**   Area: **3,000 sq. ft.**   Photographer: **Joshua McHugh**

A young entrepreneur approached the architect with the wish to have a flexible living/working environment that would also serve as a family home in the future.

Floor Plan

1. Entry	6. Study	11. Guest Bedroom
2. Library	7. Master Bedroom	12. Guest Bathroom
3. Living Area	8. Closet	13. Power Room
4. Dining Area	9. Master Bathroom	14. Mechanical Room
5. Kitchen	10. Gym	

Flower District Loft

The loft's open public areas are visually choreographed so that they can merge, compress, and expand, depending on the client's needs. Its "elasticity" allows it to expand for a large, crowded party or to contract into separate zones for more intimate gatherings and events.

A compact volume of private space houses a guest bedroom, gym, powder room, and two bathrooms, and compresses the center of the public area at the kitchen, which becomes the focal point of the loft.

Translucent screen doors mounted on aluminum frames allow the passage of light from the private core to the public areas. Their pattern, inspired by the traditional Indian *jali*, creates a shifting pattern of translucency, depending on the direction in which the light passes through the sandwiched materials.

Other prominent features include blue lacquered walls, large windows, the presence of walnut and stainless steel, and the use of stone in the bathroom.

Boesky Loft

The distinction between **public**
and **private** space was the major
concern in the design of this Tribeca loft

Architect: **Gluckman Mayner**   Location: **New York City, United States**

Completion date: **2000**   Area: **3,000 sq. ft.**   Photographer: **Mark Arbeit**

The loft was designed for a private art dealer to accommodate the display of her art collection. The shelf unit in the living area incorporates a space for the fireplace as well as for a multitude of framed photographs and drawings.

Vertical axes of light penetrate deeply into the space, illuminating white planes of plastic and sheetrock. Skylights were created throughout various points in the loft to highlight specific areas or objects.

The division of public and private space was achieved by creating two floors. The public first floor contains the living and dining areas for entertaining, a study, and a gallery space.

The upper floor includes the den, master bedroom, bathroom, and outdoor terrace.

Baron Loft

Renovated for an art director and his family, the architects focused on the **polishing** and **reduction** of elements to achieve a pure and elegant minimalist style

Architect: **Deborah Berke**   Location: **New York City, United States**

Completion date: **2000**   Area: **3,700 sq. ft.**   Photographer: **Fabien Baron**

The materials used include smooth plaster on the walls, ebonized oak floors, polished schist blocks in the bathroom, oiled walnut slabs, brushed stainless steel splashes, white glass, and white window scrims. Each of these is detailed in the most reductive manner possible.

Much of the furniture is built into the house and displays the owner's extensive art collection.

1. Study
2. Living/Dining
3. Kitchen
4. Master Bathroom
5. Master Bedroom
6. Bathroom
7. Bedrooms

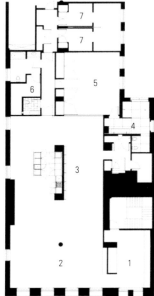

Floor Plan

A strict color palette gives way to a sober design sprinkled with subtle doses of warm tones. The kitchen is hidden behind walnut doors, while a translucent glass wall conceals the master bedroom.

All-In-One Loft

The concept of a loft can also be translated into very small spaces by employing **multifunctional** elements and a skillful **distribution** of space

Architect: **Gary Chang/EDGE (HK) Ltd.**   Location: **Hong Kong, China (SAR)**

Completion date: **2000**   Area: **320 sq. ft.**   Photographer: **Almond Chu**

1. Entry
2. Kitchen
3. Bathroom
4. Living/Bedroom
5. Studio
6. Cabinet

Floor Plan

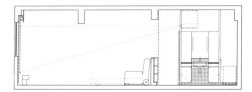

Longitudinal Section

The aim of the project was to transform the space into a home that, despite its limited proportions, would also serve as a place for leisure and entertainment. The bedroom, living room, studio, and projection room coexist in this single small space. An extendable screen offers a viewing surface for television, video, and the Internet.

In order to take advantage of the light that enters through the back window, the bathroom, kitchen, and washing areas were grouped at the front, leaving the remaining space free to incorporate a multifunctional environment. To achieve this, a combination of manipulated lighting techniques, lightweight divisions, and mobile furniture was employed.

Work elements, such as books, videos, records, and personal areas like the wardrobe, are concealed behind plain white curtains that can be easily opened or closed. Translucent white materials and changes in ambient light give the space a weightless, uncluttered feel. To enhance this effect and deepen the space vertically, fluorescent white tubes trail the floor, and intense lights accentuate structural features.

One of the few elements preserved from the original structure is the cherry wood tower that houses the projector, refrigerator, kitchen, bathroom, and washing machine.

A clever positioning of elements allows an opening in the bathroom that filters in natural light from the back window without sacrificing privacy.

CK Loft

The first floor of a former gear factory in the center of Munich, Germany became the dream-come-true for a designer couple in search of a **quiet and hidden** home inside the **city**

Architect: **Lynx Architecture**   Location: **Munich, Germany**

Completion date: **2002**   Area: **2,475 sq. ft.**   Photographer: **Andreas J. Focke**

The architects of this 2,475-square-foot loft achieved a comfortable and stylish interior by focusing their attention on space, lighting, and materials.

Floor-to-ceiling sliding panels and translucent glass walls were introduced to create a living room, bathroom, workplace, and hall.

The straightforward open-plan layout is livened up by textures along the walls and windows as well as attractive components, such as the open fireplace—a 19-foot heated marble bench that dominates the main room.

A band of light between the wall and ceiling illuminates every corner, while the artificial lighting offers a variety of "light moods" to suit the occasion.

Solid oak floors link the various areas and create a warm and comfortable surface on which to live.

The kitchen features a 14-foot island with a concrete surface and black linoleum-faced cupboards underneath.

1. Entry
2. Guest Bedroom/Study
3. Guest Bathroom
4. Kitchen
5. Living/Dining
6. Master Bedroom
7. Master Bathroom
8. Terrace

Floor Plan

In the bathroom, a large skylight was incorporated into the ceiling above the bathtub.

Marnix Warehouse
Flex House
Attic in Bilbao
Loft in Amsterdam
Composer's Loft
Pied-a-Terre

Marnix Warehouse

Dictated by the context of the project and the **identity** of their clients, these Belgian architects were hired to transform a late nineteenth-century warehouse into a **dynamic** living space

Architect: **Fokkema Architecten**   Location: **Antwerp, Belgium**

Completion date: **2000**   Area: **3,000 sq. ft.**   Photographer: **Christian Richters**

The site is located on the north edge of the city, next to a large harbor. The brick building had three major compartments with a row of oak columns running down the center. The floors were constructed out of oak beams and pine planks.

The architects attempted to reduce to a minimum all necessary elements, such as the bathrooms, bedrooms, and laundry room, in order to maximize open space and horizontal and vertical circulation.

Marnix Warehouse

The chosen scheme was to be fairly minimalist so that hectic family life could flourish and come to a rest. The idea was that the people, rather than the material, should fill up the space.

The second cube, situated halfway up the loft, contains a bedroom and the kitchen. The third cube hangs from the ceiling and contains a crow's nest bedroom.

Marnix Warehouse

Three cubes were developed: The first floats above the ground floor and contains two bathrooms. Sandblasted glass is the only barrier between the shower and the living room.

The cubes are not only functional but also mark the circulation. Cantilevered oak planks file out of one cube as a staircase that leads to the roof terrace, while another pokes through the floor and acts as the landing.

Abstract elements relate to each other in size and shape, while white plaster and sandblasted glass renew an environment of old wooden beams and columns.

Lower Floor

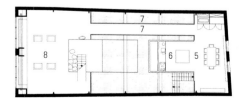

Upper Floor

1. Entry
2. Bedroom
3. Bathroom
4. Half-Bathroom
5. Dining Area
6. Kitchen
7. Bridge
8. Living Area

Flex House

The **structural** characteristics of this loft permitted architects to create a **versatile** space that adapts to the changing activities of its tenants

Architect: **Archikubik**   Location: **Barcelona, Spain**

Completion date: **2001**   Area: **1,400 sq. ft.**   Photographer: **Eugeni Pons**

The night and day zones are separated by a independent cube whose walls stop short of the ceiling, enabling unobstructed views of the wooden beams that run across the living room ceiling.

Dark translucent drapes hung from a steel cable provide an attractive contrast with the surrounding white walls and soften the industrial lines of the loft.

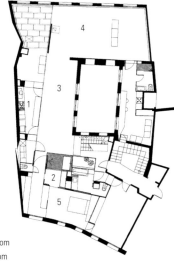

1. Kitchen
2. Bathroom
3. Dining Room
4. Living Room
5. Bedroom

Floor Plan

Light materials and mobile structures afford flexibility within an original space.
Floors were laid in concrete to create spatial continuity.

The furniture, including the tables, kitchen modules and storage closets were designed by the architects.

A red panel hangs from a railing system that runs the space longitudinally, varying the configuration of functional areas and the aesthetic perception of the design. A long table on wheels is a practical element that serves as an added work surface for the kitchen or as a dining table on its own.

The box that contains the bathroom divides the day zone and the night zone. The materials used and finishes employed inside the bathroom allow the space to integrate with either area.

Flex House

Attic in Bilbao

The aim of the project was to
give **flexibility** and **light** to a
space without leaving any obvious
traces of the intervention

Architect: **AV62 Arquitectos**   Location: **Bilbao, Spain**

Completion date: **2002**   Area: **1,180 sq. ft.**   Photographer: **Susana Aréchaga and Luís Ambrós**

The loft is situated inside an eighteenth-century building in the old section of Bilbao, Spain, and exhibits the scars of many renovations and years of weathering.

The existing framework of wood beams and structural columns were maintained, eliminating unnecessary divisions to facilitate the entry of light and the distribution of space.

The decoration is casual and practical, in keeping with the spirit of the original structure. A mild restoration and skillful layout plan render a comfortable living space full of personality.

1. Living Area
2. Dining Area
3. Kitchen
4. Bathroom
5. Bedroom

Floor Plan

An exposed layer of beams and brickwork serves as an attractive backdrop for a small music studio.

The architects introduced a container to administer all the services needed in a home: kitchen, bathroom, and storage. This cube was the determining factor of the future of the space.

An indirect lighting system makes the structure seem to levitate from the ground, reducing any perception of heaviness.

The bedroom was placed behind the cube to obtain privacy.

The bathroom is easily accessed from the bedroom or the living room, as is the storage space located on the other side of the container.

Loft in Amsterdam

Simplicity of color and
design often result in the
most attractive and **practical**
open-plan living spaces

Architect: **Dick van Gameren (De Architectengroep)**   Location: **Amsterdam, Holland**

Completion date: **2001**   Area: **3,000 sq. ft.**   Photographer: **Christian Richters**

This fully restored loft space in Amsterdam preserved its wooden beams and large facade windows and incorporates a central module that distributes the day and night areas.

The natural wood floors of the loft blend subtly with the surrounding white surfaces, broken only by the dark sofa that marks the living room.

The central unit, whose walls stop short of the ceiling to maintain spatial fluidity, incorporates a seamless series of cupboards and drawers, one of which pulls out into a dining table.

On the facade side, the kitchen installations take advantage of the light and views. A sliding translucent glass door leads into the bedroom and beyond. The opposite side of the module contains room for storage and also leads to the bedroom. It can be closed off by a series of sliding panels that hang from a railing.

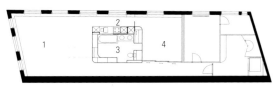

1. Living/Dining
2. Kitchen
3. Bathroom
4. Bedroom

Floor Plan

Loft in Amsterdam

The bathroom is contained within the unit; its opaque glass panel above the bathtub acts as the kitchen splash back on the other side. An opening was maintained above the bathroom to avoid humidity and to allow light to enter the space.

Composer's Loft

The design is based on the client's affinity for **nature** and Asian/Middle Eastern motifs and the **figurative** interpretation of these concepts into elements that compose the home

Architect: **Desai/Chia Studio**   Location: **New York City, United States**

Completion date: **1999**   Area: **3,000 sq. ft.**   Photographer: **Andrew Bordwin Studio**

This 3,000-square-foot loft was designed to accommodate a residence and a professional recording studio for a composer.

In the center of the loft stands a mahogany structure inspired by a Japanese bathhouse, including an open shower, concrete soaking tub, a mahogany vanity, and a changing room.

The living area is based on the layout of an Islamic courtyard garden and incorporates a water feature, which serves as a greeting and cleansing element near the entrance.

The recording studio was conceived as a "box within a box" to achieve acoustic isolation. The room incorporates high-tech audiovisual equipment and acoustically insulated panels wrapped in silk fabrics. The electronic installations throughout the loft permit the owner to record music from any room, creating a completely integrated living/working environment.

A recurring theme in Asian landscape paintings—the vision of a scholar's retreat in the woods—stimulated the design of the bedroom and library. These spaces were wrapped in custom mahogany cabinetry and linked by a large bluestone fireplace, whose open hearth can be seen from anywhere in the room.

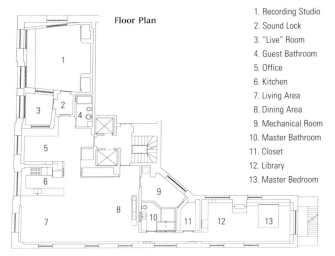

Floor Plan

1. Recording Studio
2. Sound Lock
3. "Live" Room
4. Guest Bathroom
5. Office
6. Kitchen
7. Living Area
8. Dining Area
9. Mechanical Room
10. Master Bathroom
11. Closet
12. Library
13. Master Bedroom

Composer's Loft

Stainless steel and glass windows open to provide views over Manhattan.

Pied-a-Terre

The interior of this pied-a-terre
is a response to the need for
relaxation and **escape** from
stress and the daily routine

Architect: **Belle van't Hoff**   Location: **Amsterdam, Holland**

Completion date: **2000**   Area: **900 sq. ft.**   Photographer: **Virginia del Guidice**

A humid, dark attic of an Amsterdam residence was transformed into a luminous loft for a client in search of an escape from his hectic lifestyle.

Composed of three areas, the loft's main feature is the central module that contains the bathroom, kitchen, storage area, and heating installations.

The layout is a practical scheme in which the kitchen can be concealed from the living area and the bedroom can enjoy considerable privacy.